Unsolved Mysteries

The Mysteries
of UFOs

Brian Innes

RSVP

RAINTREE
STECK-VAUGHN
P U B L I S H E R S
A Steck-Vaughn Company

Austin, Texas

Developed by Brown Partworks
Editor: Lindsey Lowe
Designer: Joan Curtis

Raintree Steck-Vaughn Publishers Staff
Project Manager: Joyce Spicer
Editor: Pam Wells

Library of Congress Cataloging-in-Publication Data
Innes, Brian.
  The mysteries of UFOs/by Brian Innes.
    p.   cm.—(Unsolved mysteries)
  Includes bibliographical references and index.
  Summary: Describes some of the sightings reported about mysterious and
sometimes unexplained objects in the skies.
  ISBN 0-8172-5477-3 (Hardcover)
  ISBN 0-8172-4274-0 (Softcover)
  1. Unidentified flying objects—Juvenile literature.
[1. Unidentified flying objects.] I. Title. II. Series: Innes, Brian. Unsolved
mysteries.
TL789.2.I53   1999
001.942—dc21   98-9354
                                                     CIP
                                                      AC

Printed and bound in the United States
1 2 3 4 5 6 7 8 9 0   WZ   02 01 00 99 98

Acknowledgments

Cover Mary Evans Picture Library;
Pages 5 and 6: Fortean Picture Library; **Page 8:**
Peregrine Mendoza/Fortean Picture Library;
Page 10: Corbis-Bettmann/UPI; **Page 11:** Mary
Evans Picture Library; **Page 13:** Charles Walker
Collection/Images Colour Library; **Page 14:** Fortean
Picture Library; **Page 16:** Hulton-Deutsch
Collection/Corbis; **Pages 17, 19, and 20:** Mary
Evans Picture Library; **Page 21:** USAF/TRH;
Pages 23, 24, and 25: Mary Evans Picture Library;
Page 27: Charles Walker Collection/Images
Colour Library; **Page 29:** Mary Evans Picture
Library; **Page 30:** Michael Ruhler/ Mary Evans
Picture Library; **Page 33:** Fortean Picture Library;
Page 35: Mary Evans Picture Library; **Pages 37
and 38:** Fortean Picture Library; **Page 41:** Julian
Baum/Science Photo Library; **Page 43:** David
Nunuk/Science Photo Library; **Page 44:** Fate
Magazine/Mary Evans Picture Library; **Page 45:**
UPI/Corbis-Bettmann.

Contents

"Flying Saucers"

Strange objects had been seen in the skies for centuries. Then, in the 1940s, the first "flying saucers" were spotted.

Kenneth Arnold was a businessman from Boise, Idaho. On the afternoon of June 24, 1947, he was flying his own small plane over the Cascade Mountains of Washington State. A Marine Corps C-46 transport plane had come down near Mount Rainier with 32 men aboard. A reward of $5,000 was offered to anyone who found it. Arnold was looking for it.

At about 3:00 P.M., a bright flash lit up the surfaces of his aircraft. Arnold's first thought was that it was an explosion, then he decided that the light might have been sunlight reflected from the wings of a jet fighter. Then came another brilliant flash. This time Arnold saw a group of very bright objects to the north. They were moving at tremendous speed, close to the mountaintops and in the direction of Mount Rainier. He reckoned that they were about 20 miles (32 km) away.

THE FIRST FLYING SAUCERS

An hour later, Arnold landed at Yakima, where he talked to several pilots. One suggested that these objects might have been guided missiles fired from a nearby test range. Arnold flew on to

The picture from Kenneth Arnold's book The Coming of the Saucers *(opposite) illustrates what he saw while out flying in 1947.*

4

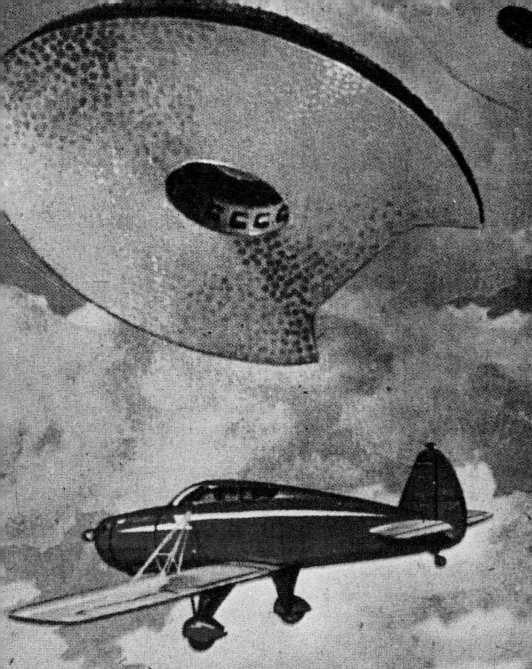

"They flew like a saucer would, if you skipped it across the water."

KENNETH ARNOLD

Pendleton, Oregon, where he was met by a crowd of newspaper reporters. Arnold searched for the right words to describe the way the mysterious objects flew. "They flew like a saucer would, if you skipped it across the water." The newsmen seized on the phrase. The "flying saucers" hit headlines everywhere. And reports of sightings began to flood in from all over the United States.

THE ROSWELL INCIDENT

Some 85 miles (136 km) to the northwest of Roswell, New Mexico, lay the Foster Ranch. It was a rough, isolated spread. It belonged to "Mac" Brazel, a rancher. On the night of June 13, 1947, the weather was stormy. But Brazel said he heard the sound of an explosion above the sound of thunder.

The remains of the "flying disk" that crashed near "Mac" Brazel's ranch on the night of June 13, 1947. Military experts said it was a weather balloon.

The following morning, June 14, he went to check his sheep. He found a trail of wreckage across his land. It was like thin metal foil, but it was very tough. He said he could not crumple it.

On July 5, Brazel was in the town of Corona. He heard about the wave of flying-saucer sightings for the first time. So he reported his find to the USAAF base at Roswell. On July 8, Major Jesse Marcel went with him to inspect the debris on his land. Many years later, in 1978, Marcel spoke of what he saw. He said it was like "nothing made on Earth."

He described how he collected the pieces. Then he loaded them into his Buick. He put them in the trunk and backseats. He said some of the pieces had strange markings on them. There was also something like light balsa wood. It had not burned.

A THRILLING STATEMENT

That same day the *Roswell Daily Record* printed an exciting story. It quoted a statement by Lt. Warren Haught, public relations officer at the base: "The many rumors regarding the flying disk became a reality yesterday, when the intelligence office of the 509th Bomb Group of the Eighth Air Force, Roswell Army Air Field, was fortunate enough to gain possession of a disk, through the cooperation [with the assistance] of one of the local ranchers, and the sheriff's office of Chaves County."

This newspaper report caused a sensation. The wreckage was flown to Air Force Headquarters at Fort Worth, Texas. There, Brigadier-General Roger Ramey went on the air. However, he denied that the remains were part of a flying saucer. The wreckage was, he said, the remains of a weather balloon.

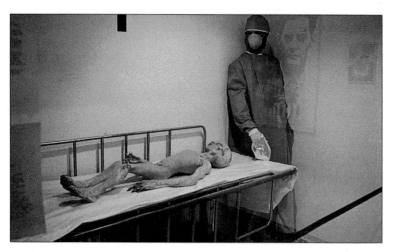

This display in the UFO museum, Roswell, New Mexico, is a setup showing the medical examination that was supposedly done on one of the dead aliens.

A meeting of the press was called. Newsmen took photographs of the wreckage, but they complained that they had not been allowed close enough. So a second meeting was held. The reporters were still not happy. They said the pieces were not the same. A rumor quickly spread that they had been switched. Later, Major Marcel said he knew what a weather balloon looked like. And that was not what he had collected at Roswell!

DEAD ALIENS

Also on July 8, another strange thing took place. Civil engineer Grady L. Barnett was out in the desert of New Mexico. He was west of Socorro, not far from the northern end of the White Sands missile range. Barnett saw what he thought might be an aircraft that had crashed, so he hurried toward it.

He was joined by some students of archaeology, who study the remains, the art and dwellings, of past human life. They were working in the area. The students found some strange wreckage. It was later described by them as "some sort of metallic, disk-shaped object." It was about 30 feet (9 m) across. It was split open and inside were a number of bodies. Other bodies were lying on the ground beside it. They were ". . . like humans. But they were not humans. The heads were round. The eyes were small, and they had no hair. The eyes were oddly spaced. They were quite small by our standards. Their heads were larger, in proportion [when compared] to their bodies, than ours." They wore gray coveralls, without belts or zippers.

Barnett told friends about his discovery. But he died later. His friends said he told them what had happened. Military personnel had arrived and roped off the area. They told the civilians it was "their patriotic duty" to say nothing about the crash.

"[They were] . . . like humans. But they were not humans. . . ."

WITNESSES AT THE SCENE OF A POSSIBLE UFO CRASH

The Brazel story and the Barnett story have been combined, and together are now known as the "Roswell Incident." They came at the time of the first great wave of flying-saucer sightings. So they caused great public concern. There was suspicion that the military authorities had tried to hide the evidence. Over the years such rumors have grown. At that time, the craft were called flying saucers. Later such things came to be called "Unidentified Flying Objects" (UFOs), which is a more scientific term.

More than 30 years after the Roswell Incident, a book was written about it. The author claimed that the alien bodies were being kept secret in a CIA warehouse. This warehouse was at Langley, Virginia. A film has been made recently that is supposed to show a medical examination taking place on one of the bodies. But most people believe this to be a fake.

Because of the constant rumors about what happened at Roswell, an Air Force investigation was undertaken in 1994. This revealed that a top secret operation, Project Mogul, was begun in 1947. This involved strings of hot-air balloons designed to keep an eye on any Soviet nuclear tests. The balloons were made from balsa wood, reflective silver material, and pink-patterned tape! In June 1947, the balloons had been tracked to the Roswell area, before disappearing from the radar screen. Despite such a convincing explanation, Roswell believers refuse to accept this evidence. They maintain that it is just another cover-up, particularly since the report "did not address the issue of alien bodies."

DEATH IN THE SKY

Concern about flying saucers was fed by a tragedy that occurred a few months after Roswell, on January 7, 1948. It happened in Kentucky, not long after midday. Several people saw an object in the sky. It was huge, some 250 feet (75 m) wide. It was moving very fast. One observer described it as looking like "an ice cream cone topped with red."

Captain Thomas F. Mantell. He was killed while chasing a UFO in his fighter plane on January 7, 1948.

In 1949, several people claimed to have spotted a flying saucer in the sky during the launching of one of the U.S. Navy's Project Skyhook balloons.

The object was also seen at the Godman Air Force Base, near Fort Knox. Three F-51 Mustang fighters were sent to follow the object. One of the pilots reported it was "of tremendous size." It appeared to be made of metal, "round like a teardrop, and at times almost fluid." Two of the pilots pulled out of the chase. But Captain Mantell radioed: "I'm going to 20,000 feet [6,000 m]. If I'm no closer then, I'll abandon." That was the last heard from him. Later, his body was found in the wreck of his plane some 80 miles (128 km) to the southwest. An Air Force report concluded that he had blacked out through lack of oxygen at around 20,000 feet (6,000 m).

It was suggested that the object was the planet Venus. Others said it was a balloon. The U.S. Navy had been experimenting with balloons for use high above the Earth—the program was called Project Skyhook. People refused to accept this explanation. Many believed Mantell had been attacked by a UFO.

Visions of the Heavens

Can all strange flying objects in the sky really be visitors from outer space?

There are many accounts of fiery objects being seen in the sky. They are often described as dragons. Matthew Paris, an English historian, described seeing "a great star like a torch" that appeared in western England on July 24, 1239. "It was shaped like a great head. The front part was sparkling. And the back part gave out smoke and flashes. It turned to the north, not quickly, but exactly as if it wished to ascend [climb] to a place in the air."

The Duke of Burgundy of France described another sighting in his memoirs. He wrote: "On November 1, 1461, appeared in the sky an object as bright as a bar of iron, as long and wide as a half moon. It hung . . . for about a quarter hour, clearly visible. Then suddenly the strange object . . . twisted and turned, like a spring, and rose into the heavens."

This drawing (opposite) was based on sightings of the "Great Airship" UFO that sailed over the U.S. during the fall of 1896.

BATTLE IN THE SKIES

The skies over the old city of Nuremberg, Germany, once played host to an astonishing vision. Above their heads, observers saw a fierce battle. It was on the morning of April 4, 1561. There were two huge black tubes. Out of these

"Nobody has ever fully explained a wave of 'airship' sightings in the U.S."

tubes came blue, black, and red balls, blood-red crosses, and disk shapes. The battle went on for about an hour. A similar battle was to take place in the skies above Basel, a town in Switzerland, five or six years later.

MYSTERIOUS SIGHTS

By the 18th century, astronomers—people who study the stars and planets—had made big discoveries. They start-

Large blue, black, orange, and red globes were seen in the skies over Basel, Switzerland, in 1566. There has never been a satisfactory explanation for this event.

ed to explain many things. But they still could not explain everything they saw in the skies.

On the evening of October 18, 1783, a man called Tiberio Cavallo was watching the sky. He was standing on the terrace of Windsor Castle, in southern England. This is one of the homes that belongs to the British royal family. The sky was clear. Suddenly, Cavallo saw a large, square-shaped cloud. It was moving along the horizon. Under it was a bright globe. The globe stopped moving. At first its light was pale blue, then it began to glow intensely.

The globe moved again. It was changing direction. Cavallo said the strange object gave out a brilliant light and lit up everything on the ground. Then it changed its shape. It seemed to separate into two parts. "A sort of trail appeared." Two minutes later, he heard the sound of a huge explosion. Nobody was able to explain this event at the time.

During the 19th century, knowledge grew rapidly. Scientists were quick to dismiss reports of strange objects. They explained everything as being either a "meteor" or a balloon. A meteor is made up of small particles that float about in the solar system. They can be seen from Earth because they glow.

A BLACK SAUCER?

Balloons were a new and unfamiliar sight in the sky. Perhaps that was what John Martin saw toward the end of the 19th century. Or perhaps it wasn't!

John Martin was a farmer near Denison, Texas. On January 2, 1878, he was out hunting when he saw a dark object in the sky to the north. When he first saw it, it was small. It appeared to be about the size of an orange. It moved "at a wonderful speed" and at a great height. Then it was directly above him. At this point Martin described it as being the size of "a large saucer." This object appeared to be black, but this is probably because it was against the light sky behind it. What it was remains a mystery.

"... the strange object gave out a brilliant light and lit up everything on the ground."

SENSATIONAL HEADLINES

Nobody has ever fully explained a wave of "airship" sightings in the U.S. They happened in 1896–97 over California, the Midwest, and Texas and made front-page news. Many of them, without doubt, were accounts of hoaxes, or tricks. What is certain is that nobody reported anything like a flying saucer. Nor did anyone see bright objects moving at high speed. All the descriptions were of cigar-shaped craft with propellers. They sound like experimental power-driven airships, which were being built at that time in the U.S. and in Europe.

"FOO FIGHTERS"

In 1966–67 Sir Francis Chichester became a famous sailor. He was honored for his single-handed voyage around the world. But earlier in life he was a pioneer flier. In 1931, he made the first solo flight from Australia to New Zealand. During the flight Chichester was puzzled. He saw flashing lights in the sky. They zigzagged at high speed. He wrote that one was "like a silver pearl." It was flashing like a searchlight and came close to his plane.

Sir Francis Chichester in the cockpit of his plane in 1930, a year before his encounter with "foo fighters."

Chichester's flashing lights seem to be like the "foo fighters" that later worried USAAF pilots all over Europe during World War II. Reports flooded in during the fall of 1944. Pilots saw balls of light. They said they suddenly appeared out of nowhere. Some were red; others were bright orange or white. They seemed to "play" with the airplanes, diving and darting in the sky around them. There were as many as ten at

This photograph of a UFO was taken in Sweden in 1946. Could it have been an ordinary aircraft?

one time. Sometimes the lights blinked on and off.

"Foo fighters" got their name from the "Smokey Stover" comic strip. One of the characters in the comic strip had a favorite saying: "Where there's foo, there's fire." The pilots thought that the "foo fighters" were a German secret weapon. But no planes were harmed. Later, many German pilots said that they had also seen them. They thought they were a U.S. secret weapon!

UNNATURAL HAPPENINGS

World War II had been over for a year by the summer of 1946. Nevertheless, people began to report "ghost rockets" in the sky. The sightings were in northern Sweden and Finland. On July 19, one "rocket" fell into Lake Kölmjärv, Sweden. It exploded. Around 1,000 sightings were reported over seven months in Sweden alone. At first, the Soviets were suspected. It was thought they had been experimenting with captured German V2 rockets. This was denied by the Soviets.

In October, the Swedish Defense Ministry said 80 percent of the sightings had been identified and explained as ordinary aircraft. However, some 200 sightings remained a mystery.

Unidentified Flying Objects

With reported sightings of flying saucers on the increase, the U.S. authorities decided to step in.

Sightings of UFOs increased steadily following the Roswell Incident in 1947. As a result, the U.S. government in Washington became worried that there might be a threat to national safety. A project code-named "Sign" was set up. It had orders to look into all sightings of "unidentified flying objects," or UFOs.

After Captain Thomas Mantell's fatal crash in early 1948, the Pentagon decided Project Sign needed more expert advice. They enlisted the help of professor J. Allen Hynek from Ohio State University.

SENSIBLE EXPLANATIONS

Every few weeks Dr. Hynek would read his way through a pile of sighting reports. He would say: "Well, this is obviously a meteor." Or he would say: "This is not a meteor. But I'll bet you it's a balloon." He believed every sighting had to have a natural explanation. But he found it difficult to explain what happened on July 23, 1948.

Captain C. S. Chiles and his copilot J. B. Whitted were flying a transport plane from Houston, Texas, to Boston, Massachusetts. At

On August 30, 1951, Carl Hart took four photographs of a formation of UFOs (opposite). They have never been satisfactorily explained.

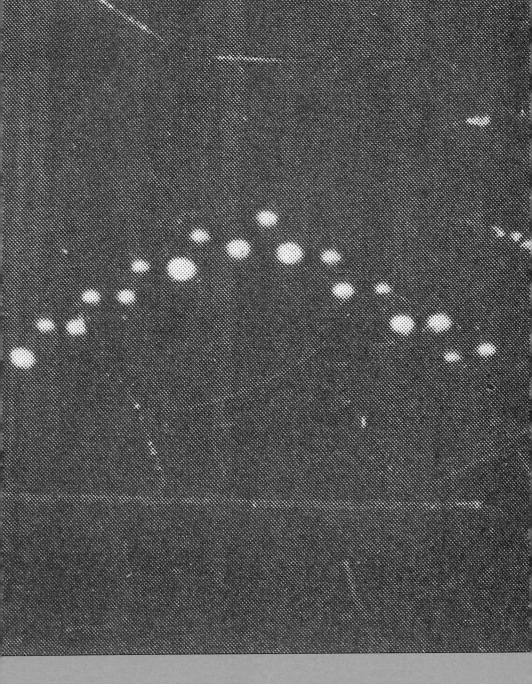

"... they clearly showed a V-shaped flight pattern consisting of about 20 lights."

Despite disbelievers, the Condon Committee finally declared that Mrs. Trent's photograph of a UFO was real.

2:45 A.M. they were at 5,000 feet (1,500 m) when they saw a glowing red light coming straight toward them. Horrified, they banked sharply to the left. The object passed the right wing less than 100 feet (30 m) away, then it climbed steeply. There was a burst of orange flame, then it disappeared. Chiles and Whitted said it looked like an aircraft without wings. It appeared to have rows of "windows" along the side that glowed with a bright light.

Dr. Hynek decided it must have been a particle of space matter, but some of the staff members of Project Sign disagreed. They wrote an unofficial report. In it they made the daring suggestion that some of the UFOs might not come from Earth. The report reached the Air Force Chief of Staff, General Hoyt S. Vandenberg. He rejected it and ordered the destruction of all copies. Early in 1949, Project Sign was officially abandoned.

PHOTOGRAPHS OF A UFO

Those who did not believe in UFOs wondered why nobody had taken a good photograph. Then, on May 11, 1950, a farmer and his wife produced two. The farmer's name was Paul Trent, and he lived near McMinnville, Oregon. His wife was outside feeding her rabbits. It was about 7:30 P.M. She saw a bright, silvery disk in the sky. It was silently gliding toward her. She called for her husband and ran to get a camera. The Trents managed to take two photographs. Then the object flew out of sight.

A local newspaper printed the photographs about a month later, but many people said they were pictures of a model hung from a string. However, much later the Condon Committee, a government study of UFOs set up in the 1960s, concluded that the photographs were real.

HARD EVIDENCE

The Air Force attempted to expose UFO reports as fakes. But it could not explain all the reports. On the evening of August 25, 1951, three people in Albuquerque saw a huge craft pass silently overhead. The craft was V-shaped, and eight soft blue lights glowed from it. Twenty minutes later 20–30 soft blue lights, flying in a crescent-shaped grouping, were seen over Lubbock, Texas.

On August 31, college freshman Carl Hart came forward. He had four photographs that he presented to the *Lubbock Evening Avalanche.* Taken the previous night, they clearly showed a V-shaped group of about 20 lights. One explanation was that the lights came from an experimental jet bomber called the Northrop YB-49 "flying wing." But this was never confirmed.

During 1952 there were 1,500 reports of UFO sightings. The Air Force decided to create "Project Blue Book" to check them out.

The experimental Northrop YB-49 jet. It was first flown on October 21, 1947.

Project Blue Book

Project Blue Book was set up to look into UFOs in 1952. In that year alone there had been over 1,500 sightings.

An artist's impression (opposite) of the scene at the Andrews Air Force Base, Maryland, when UFOs were spotted over Washington, D.C., on July 26, 1952.

In its first year Project Blue Book was busy. In June 1952, there were 150 reports of UFOs. Before that they had come in at 10–20 per month. In July 1952, there were 536! And there were 50 reports on just one day—July 28. There were fewer in August—326. After that the figures leveled off to about 50 a month.

THREATENED CAPITOL

Washington, D.C., was the scene of intense dramatic activity at 11:40 P.M. on July 19, 1952. Unexplained "blips" had appeared on two radar screens at National Airport, just a few miles from the White House.

The USAF Defense Command was notified. (The Air Force became a force separate from the Army at the end of 1947 and became known as the USAF, where before it had been the USAAF.) Across the Potomac River lay Andrews Air Force Base in Maryland. Radar controllers there reported a similar contact. Observers reported a large orange globe that seemed to be hovering over the base. Airline pilots were also calling by radio. They reported strange lights in the sky near the Capitol.

22

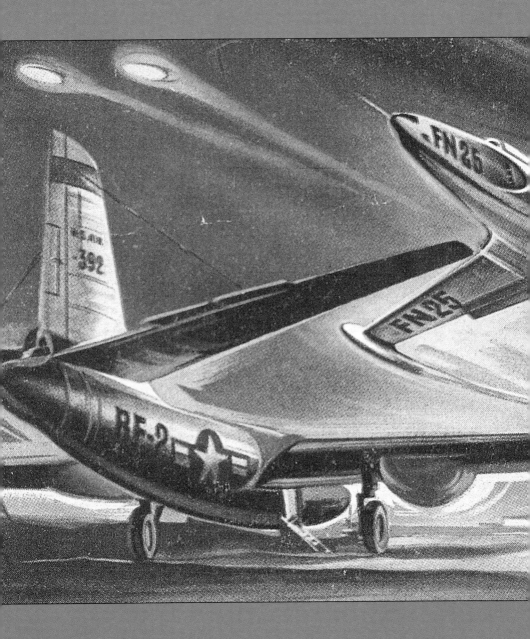

"... the Air Force sent up another pair of F-49s. This time the UFOs were visible on their radar screens."

In 1957, a UFO was detected on the radar screen of this B-47 jet bomber. It was then observed following the plane (arrowed above, and in close-up inset).

A week later the UFOs returned. It was 10:30 P.M. on July 26. They moved in the same way. Radar at National Airport and Andrews Base picked them up again. At 11:25 P.M., two F-49 fighter jets came roaring over Washington. The blips on the radar vanished. The jets searched the sky for 10 minutes, then headed back home. The UFOs reappeared. At 3:20 A.M., the Air Force sent up another pair of F-49s. This time the UFOs were visible on their radar screens. Lt. William Patterson found himself surrounded by a ring of enormous blue-white lights. He radioed the base for permission to fire and waited for his controllers to respond. Before they did, the lights flew off at high speed.

CHASING UFOs

Around 4:00 A.M. on July 17, 1957, a Boeing B-47 jet bomber was over the Gulf of Mexico on a routine exercise. The sky was clear. The bomber was turning for home over Gulfport, Mississippi, when the radar operator saw a blip on his screen. Something was coming close. It was near the right-hand side of the plane. He watched the object. It appeared to climb rapidly in front of the bomber. Then it moved along the left side. It was as if the object was circling the jet. A few minutes later, at 4:10 A.M., the pilot and copilot became alarmed. They saw a brilliant blue-white light racing at high speed toward them. It looked as if it was going to hit them. Then it changed direction and disappeared. The pilot said later it was "as big as a barn." The bomber's equipment continued to pick up strong signals that lasted for more than eight minutes.

At 4:39 A.M., the bomber was approaching Fort Worth, Texas. The light appeared again about 5,000 feet (1,500 m) below. It was just off to the right. It was also visible once more on the radar. Then the two pilots saw a glowing red object.

Project Blue Book in 1967. The group, headed by Major Hector Quintanilla (center), was unable to deal with the huge numbers of UFO reports. The office was closed two years later.

25

The ground operator at Fort Worth said he had the bomber on his radar. The UFO was also there. The pilot asked for permission to chase it. Ground control gave it. The bomber began diving toward the light, which was moving at around 550 miles per hour (880 km per hour).

GAME OF CAT AND MOUSE

The radar continued to show the UFO. It was moving swiftly away from the plane. Then, at 4:50 A.M., it no longer moved. It seemed that it suddenly stopped still in the air.

The bomber could do nothing but race past. The pilot brought his plane around. Then the light came in sight again two minutes later.

"They saw a brilliant blue-white light racing at high speed toward them."

Again the pilot lost contact with the object. It was like a cat chasing a mouse. Six minutes later, the object was picked up once more, 20 miles (32 km) northwest of Fort Worth. At last, as the jet bomber drew near Oklahoma City, the light vanished. Its radar signal faded away. The plane returned to base. It had pursued the UFO for 700 miles (1,120 km) across four states.

Air Force officials and Project Blue Book were in agreement. All said the visual sighting, and the radar trace, had come from the same source. But they announced that this source was a passenger plane!

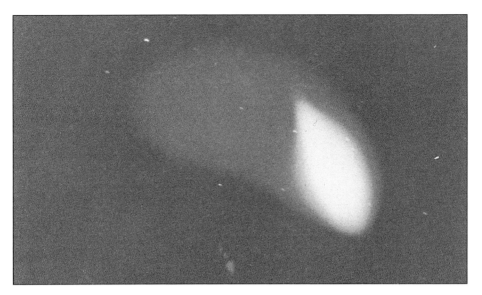

This photograph of a UFO was taken in January 1971. By then, however, Project Blue Book had been closed down. This sighting, as with many others, has never been explained.

UFO CENTER FOUNDED

Project Blue Book was unable to deal with the thousands of UFO reports that came in over the years. Finally, in 1969, Blue Book was closed down. The public, however, was unhappy. People felt that UFO sightings did not get the attention they deserved. Several unofficial organizations were set up. One was the National Investigations Committee on Aerial Phenomena (NICAP). Many of its board members were said to be CIA agents.

Dr. J. Allen Hynek, who had been in charge of a UFO investigation project in the late 1940s code-named "Sign," felt there was not enough scientific investigation of UFOs, so he set up the Center for UFO Studies (CUFOS). In 1973, NICAP was dissolved. All its files were transferred to CUFOS. Hynek died in 1986, and CUFOS was renamed the J. Allen Hynek Center. It still exists today.

27

Close Encounters

J. Allen Hynek, founder of the Center for UFO Studies (CUFOS), classified close encounters, or unexpected meetings, with UFOs. He said there were five kinds of encounters: Close Encounters of the First Kind, when UFOs are clearly seen and described; Close Encounters of the Second Kind, where UFOs produce physical effects on humans, animals, and objects; Close Encounters of the Third Kind, when beings are seen in or near UFOs; Close Encounters of the Fourth Kind, when humans are taken aboard a UFO; and Close Encounters of the Fifth Kind, in which humans contact UFOs by conventional signals, or by telepathy, communication by thought.

A HARMFUL VISION

One of the most distressing encounters of the Second Kind occurred on December 29, 1980. It happened near Dayton, Texas. Betty Cash, Vickie Landrum, and Vickie's young grandson Colby were driving home. It was about 9:00 P.M. Colby pointed out a bright light above the trees some three miles ahead. They got closer, then saw a UFO blocking the road.

Missionary William Gill and 37 natives saw a disk with waving occupants (opposite) hovering over the mission in Papua New Guinea, in June 1959.

"As we watched it, men came out from this object and appeared on top of it."

REVEREND WILLIAM GILL

Vickie later described the UFO as being "like a dia-mond of fire." It had a ring of blue lights around its center. It stopped directly above the road and sent down blasts of fiery exhaust. The light illuminated the surrounding woods.

All three got out of the car. Then Colby became frightened. He begged his grandmother to get back into the car with him. But Betty remained out front. It was as if she was in a trance. The heat from the UFO was burning her skin, but she did not seem to notice. Suddenly there were heli-copters overhead. "They seemed to rush in from all directions," Betty reported. "It seemed like they were trying to encircle the thing." The women watched the UFO and the helicopters for some 20 minutes. In all, they counted 23 helicopters, which they later iden-tified as CH-47 Chinooks.

AFTEREFFECTS

At about 9:50 P.M. Betty dropped Vickie and Colby at their home. She felt too ill to talk to her fami-

An artist's impression of Vickie Landrum, her grandson Colby, and their encounter of the Second Kind on December 29, 1980.

ly when she reached her own home. Over the next few hours her skin turned red, as if she was badly sun-burned. Her neck swelled, and blisters broke out on her face, eyelids, and scalp. Vickie and Colby also suf-fered similar symptoms.

Betty's condition worsened. She had to be admit-ted to the hospital, where she was treated for burns. At first the staff were not told about the UFO. "It was just too crazy to mention," said Vicky. The symptoms were like those of severe sunburn. All three were feverish and had bad headaches. Finally Colby told a doctor what had happened.

Within a few weeks their health worsened. Their hair started falling out. Vickie feared she might go blind. Betty's skin erupted, leaving her with large scars. Doctors guessed the cause. They believed that all three had been exposed to radiation and treated them for radiation sickness.

Houston International Airport was contacted. It could provide no information about the UFO or the helicopters. Questions were asked at the U.S. Army's Fort Hood. No helicopters from the base were in the Houston area on December 29. All other bases in Texas and Louisiana denied involvement.

Vickie and Betty brought law suits against the U.S. government. They wanted $20 million damages. But the case was eventually dismissed. The grounds for dismissal were that no government agency owned or operated any flying machine like the one described by Betty, Vickie, and Colby.

FACT OR FICTION?

There have been many reports of encounters of the Third Kind. One dramatic incident was reported by George Adamski. It happened on November 20, 1952. Adamski went out into the California desert with six companions. They hoped to see a UFO.

They were eating a picnic lunch. Then, claimed Adamski, they saw a UFO: "Riding high, and without sound, there was a gigantic cigar-shaped silvery ship." He grabbed a couple of cameras. Then he set off along a dirt road. A short way up the road he noticed a figure standing about 450 yards (410 m) away. It looked like a man at the entrance to a ravine. He was waving, so Adamski went closer.

Adamski wrote about his experience later. The man was about 5 feet 6 inches (1.65 m) tall. He weighed about 135 lbs. (61 kg). He seemed some 30 years old and had shoulder-length, sandy hair. His eyes were "calm, gray-green" and slanted slightly at the corners. He was wearing a one-piece, chocolate-brown suit with a wide belt. There were no visible fasteners or pockets.

Adamski claimed the being communicated with him. It used a mixture of sign language and mind communication. His name was Orthon and he came from the planet Venus. His spacecraft had come to Earth to try to stop the testing of atomic weapons.

Adamski first wrote about his encounter as if it were a science-fiction story. Later it was rewritten as the truth in a book called *Flying Saucers Have Landed*.

"Riding high, and without sound, there was a gigantic cigar-shaped silvery ship."

GEORGE ADAMSKI

GLORY FROM ABOVE

Reverend William Gill told a more likely tale. He was a missionary based in Papua New Guinea, in the South Pacific. His account was one of a total of 79 reports of a UFO that had been sighted in the area. And he observed the event with 37 other people on the evening of June 26, 1959.

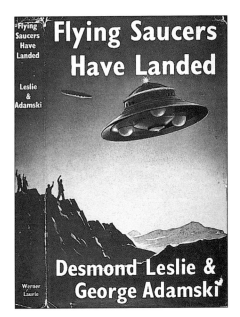

In 1953, George Adamski wrote a book about his "Close Encounter of the Third Kind" with Orthon, a visitor from the planet Venus.

Reverend Gill could see the planet Venus in the sky. Above it was "this sparkling object." Soon it came down toward the mission. Gill and his companions saw that it was circular with a narrower upper deck.

"As we watched it, men came out from this object and appeared on top of it. There were four men in all. A shaft of blue light shone from what appeared to be the center of the deck. The men appeared to be illuminated—not only by this light reflected on them, but also by a sort of glow which completely surrounded them, as well as the craft." Clouds gradually covered the sky. But the UFO remained visible below them. Then it disappeared from sight. Later it was seen "coming and going through the clouds." It finally vanished shortly before a heavy rainstorm, which began at 11:00 P.M.

The following evening the UFO returned. Again figures appeared on its upper deck. "One appeared to be standing looking down on us. . . ." Reverend Gill raised his arm and waved. To his astonishment, the figure waved back. One of his companions then waved both arms. Two of the figures did the same!

At 10:40 P.M. Gill made a note: "A terrific explosion just outside the mission house. Nothing seen." The following night eight objects appeared high in the sky. This time no figures could be seen. After that, peace returned to the mission house.

Men in Black

Strange things can happen to people who see UFOs. Many are visited by mysterious men who dress in black.

On June 21, 1947, Harold Dahl was in a U.S. Coast Guard launch patrolling Puget Sound, in Washington State. With him was his 15-year-old son, another man, and a dog. Suddenly they spotted six "large, doughnut-shaped machines" directly overhead.

One of these UFOs appeared to be in trouble. Meanwhile the others circled. Dahl said it was about 100 feet (30 m) wide. The hole in the middle was about 25 feet (7.5 m) across. It was made of shiny metal, and there were portholes around the outside.

BEACH ATTACK

Dahl landed on the beach at Maury Island. Then he took four photographs of the UFO. Suddenly it dropped some molten metal fragments onto the beach. One killed the dog. Another burned Dahl's son badly. The two men gathered up some of the fragments and returned to base, where Dahl told his boss, Fred L. Crisman, what had happened.

Early the following morning, Dahl was visited by a mysterious man wearing a black suit. He arrived at Dahl's home in a black Buick

Are the sinister "Men in Black" (opposite) really aliens pretending to be official investigators?

"Silence is the best thing for you. . . . You have seen what you ought not to have seen."

A MAN IN BLACK

sedan. The man said to Dahl: "Silence is the best thing for you and your family. You have seen what you ought not to have seen."

On June 23, Crisman developed Dahl's photographs. He said they were covered in white spots. It was "as though they had been exposed to some radiation." On June 25, news of Kenneth Arnold's UFO sighting near Mount Rainier was in all the newspapers. Crisman spoke to a local reporter. The report was passed on to Arnold.

On June 30, Arnold arrived in Tacoma to speak to Crisman. The following day Crisman contacted Lt. Frank Brown, an intelligence officer at Hamilton USAAF Base, California. Lt. Brown and a Captain Davidson flew up to Washington immediately.

DEATH AND DISASTER

Brown said he had to return to Hamilton that night, but he filled a cardboard carton with the metal fragments. Twenty minutes after takeoff, the plane caught fire and crashed. Brown and Davidson died. The carton of fragments was lost.

Crisman disappeared. With him went the photographs. Dahl said he thought Crisman had left town on business. Others said they saw him boarding an Army plane headed for Alaska. It was rumored that Dahl's son had also disappeared. However, a very different version of the story was unearthed in 1987 by UFO investigator John Keel.

Keel discovered that Dahl and Crisman were not Coast Guards. They owned an old boat that they used to move lumber around Tacoma Harbor. Keel also found out that Crisman knew Ray Palmer, a publisher of a number of science-fiction magazines.

On June 25, Crisman had heard about the Arnold sighting. He "cooked up" his story with Dahl and telephoned Palmer, who arranged for Arnold to go to Tacoma. Brown and Davidson arrived and immediately realized the story was a hoax (trick). So they set out to return to California. After the fatal plane crash, Crisman and Dahl were worried that they would be held responsible. So they made a confession to the USAAF, which made Crisman leave town.

STRANGE COINCIDENCE

But something did happen at Maury Island. Dahl had been on the beach. The dog was killed, and Dahl's son was burned. He had not disappeared—he was in the hospital. But if there had been no UFOs, what had killed the dog and caused the son's injury, and who was the mysterious man in black? Keel decided to investigate further.

He discovered that something had, indeed, happened, but on June 23, not June 21. Several planes were flying over Maury Island. They were from the Atomic Energy Commission's (AEC) plutonium—a radioactive material—processing plant at Hanford in Washington State. They were carrying radioactive waste that was to be dumped far out in the ocean. However, one of the planes got into difficulty and had to drop the waste inshore instead. Dahl's photographs were genuinely spoiled by radiation.

Albert Bender was also visited by Men in Black. Were they more security agents?

Keel also explained the mysterious "man in black." It seems he was a security agent from the AEC. He did not want news about the illegal dumping of nuclear waste to get out. As far as the AEC was concerned, Crisman's exciting story had saved the day.

A FRIGHTENING VISIT

Albert Bender was head of the International Flying Saucer Bureau, an enthusiasts' amateur organization in Connecticut. He also produced a regular UFO magazine called *Space Review*. In 1953, he suddenly announced

Albert Bender's sketch of one of the three men who visited his home in September 1953.

"I know what the saucers are!" He planned to publish the answer in his magazine, but he first mailed a copy of his report to a friend.

A few days later three shadowy figures entered Bender's bedroom: "All of them were dressed in black clothes. They looked like clergymen, but wore hats similar to homburg style. The faces were not clearly discernible [easy to see]. The hats partly hid and shaded them. The eyes of all three figures suddenly lit up like flashlight bulbs. And all these seemed focused on me." One of the visitors was carrying Bender's report. He told him it was true, but that he was to close down his bureau and stop producing his magazine. He was also ordered not to tell anyone the truth "on his honor as an American citizen."

SIMILAR DESCRIPTIONS

This description sounds like a scene from an old black-and-white "B-movie." And that is part of the mystery. Many other people who are not connected with one another in any way have told stories like Bender's. The visitors look, and behave, like the "G-men" of old movies. These were FBI agents who wore dark suits and hats, black shoes and socks. Their shirts, however, were usually extremely white, as if they had just been purchased.

"All of them were dressed in black clothes. They looked like clergymen. . . ."

ALBERT BENDER

The Men in Black are often described as being "foreign." They do not smile, or frown, and are very formal. Their movements are stiff and awkward. They seem hardly human. Occasionally, the visitors are in uniform. Often it is a U.S. Air Force uniform. Some produce identity cards, but if their names are checked they turn out to be false.

LEAVING NO TRACE

Colonel George Freeman was Pentagon spokesman for the USAF's Project Blue Book. In February 1967, he spoke to UFO investigator John Keel. Freeman told Keel that: "Mysterious men dressed in Air Force uniforms, or . . . from government agencies, have been 'silencing' UFO witnesses. We have checked a number of these cases. And these men are not connected with the Air Force in any way. We haven't been able to find out anything about these men. By posing as Air Force officers and government agents they are committing a Federal offense. We would sure like to catch one. Unfortunately the trail is always too cold by the time we hear about these cases. But we're still trying."

"We would sure like to catch one. . . ."

COLONEL GEORGE FREEMAN

VICIOUS THREATS

Robert Richardson of Toledo, Ohio, had a typical experience. In July 1967, his car crashed into a UFO. He was driving at night and came around a bend to find a strange object blocking the road. Almost immediately, the UFO vanished. However, Richardson found a small piece of metal on the road.

Three days later, at 11:00 P.M., two young men came to Richardson's home. They wanted to know about the incident. Then, they drove off in a black 1953 Cadillac. He got the license plates checked. The number had not yet been issued! A week passed, then two different men arrived. They were in a current model Dodge. They both wore black suits. One spoke perfect English. The other had an accent. They asked him to give them the piece of metal. Richardson told them that it had gone for analysis. One said: "If you want your wife to stay as pretty as she is, then you'd better get the metal back."

In 1975, Carlos de Los Santos also met some Men in Black. He was driving to a television studio in

Mexico to give an interview about his recent sighting of a UFO. He said he was stopped by some men in two large, black limousines. They wore black suits. One was "Scandinavian" in appearance. He told de Los Santos: "Look, boy, if you value your life, and your family's too, don't talk any more about this sighting of yours."

ALIENS IN HUMAN FORM

People have studied such events. Because the U.S. authorities deny that the Men in Black are military or government agents, experts have come to two conclusions. The first is that the witnesses have made up the whole thing. The second is that these strangers are not human. Some people believe the strangers are aliens who have tried to look like humans, but who have not quite succeeded.

In 1986–87, Belleville, Wisconsin, was plagued by UFO sightings. This photo is a reconstruction, but a real sighting might cause a visit from the Men in Black.

Are They Real?

Do people imagine UFOs, or are they real? And if they are real, what are they?

A lenticular cloud gets its name from its lenslike, or saucerlike, shape. Unusual cloud effects, such as this lenticular cloud at sunset (opposite), may account for some UFO sightings.

Strange objects have been reported in the skies for centuries. Many were comets, planets, or strange cloud effects. Later they were airships. But a large number of objects remain a mystery.

In 1956, Captain Ruppelt, then head of Project Blue Book, tried to explain some UFO sightings. He said that when World War II ended, the Germans had several types of aircraft under development. The majority were in the earliest stages of design. But they were the only known craft that could match the fast-moving objects reported by UFO observers.

PROJECT SAUCER

One particularly special German aircraft was called "Project Saucer." It had been designed by Rudolf Schriever in 1941, and had its first test flight in June 1942. It had a dome-shaped cockpit. Around this was a wide circular ring.

Work began on a larger version at the BMW plant near Prague, Czechoslovakia (now the Czech Republic). Its propeller engines were replaced with jets set in a circular wing. It was some 140 feet (42 m) across. The craft could reach an altitude of 40,000 feet (12,000 m). It

"Many were comets, planets, or strange cloud effects."

had a speed approaching 1,250 miles per hour (2,000 km per hour). This saucer was built during the summer of 1944. It was ready for testing in 1945. Then the Allied forces arrived and captured the factories in Prague.

Dr. Wernher von Braun was head of German rocket research at Peenemünde. At the end of the war he was brought to the U.S. to help in space research. He helped to develop the Saturn rockets for the *Apollo* space program. Other German scientists may also have played key roles in developing U.S. space technology.

In 1953 Fate *magazine announced that a Canadian company, AVRO, had designed and built a "flying saucer."*

BOLD EXPERIMENTS

In 1953, the Canadian government announced that they had tried to build a huge disk-shaped aircraft. Not having the necessary technology at the time, they passed the designs to the U.S. But research into disk-shaped aircraft continued in Canada. A smaller saucer was developed at the Avro-Canada plant in Malton, Ontario. On February 16, 1953, the Canadian minister for defense claimed it would be capable of flying at 1,500 miles per hour (2,400 km per hour). He also said it would be able to climb vertically. However, the project was officially dropped in 1960. The experimental "Avro Car" is now in the USAF museum at Fort Eustis, Virginia.

Other experimental aircraft were in the skies during the 1940s and 1950s. In 1950, the U.S. Navy released a few details of the "Flying Flapjack." This was a circular aircraft able to rise almost vertically. A later model was the XF-5-U-1. This was rumored to be over 100 feet (30 m) across. It had jet nozzles set all around its rim. The speed and handling of the plane were controlled by the jets. It was round, smooth, and was built in three layers. The central layer contained the jets. It was bigger than the other two. This gave it a distinct "flying saucer" shape. And the exhaust from the jets would have looked unusual, like a bright round window. Many UFO observers had reported seeing glowing windows.

TOP SECRET

All this evidence leads to one suggestion—people who saw UFOs actually saw experimental aircraft. One item of top-secret research has been made public since Operation Desert Shield during the Gulf War of 1990–91. This is the F-117A Stealth fighter. This black aircraft is almost invisible to radar. It has a low

profile and a raised central cockpit. Because of this, the jet F-117A Stealth fighter can resemble a flying saucer during flight. It might have been mistaken for a UFO. However, this fact cannot account for all sightings of UFOs across the world.

So do UFOs really come from another civilization, another planet,

An F-117A Stealth fighter plane photographed while being refueled in midair somewhere over Kansas on August 19, 1990.

or another galaxy? Space exploration has studied the major planets in our solar system. It has proved they cannot support life. There are no astronauts from Mars or Venus circling Earth. In 1997 astronomers discovered that primitive life might exist on one of Jupiter's moons. But there is no evidence of beings with superior scientific knowledge.

"So do UFOs . . . come from another civilization, another planet, or another galaxy?"

Could UFOs actually come from much farther out in space? It has been suggested that aliens could come from the star group known as the Pleiades. But it would take an astronaut from Earth nearly seven million years to reach Pleiades. Science fiction has the answer. Astronauts travel vast distances by "warping" space-time. But this is still fiction, although physicists can imagine something like this happening.

Some scientists have suggested another possibility. They believe an endless number of universes might exist side by side. The events in one universe are different from those in another. But perhaps a spacecraft from one universe might be able to cross over and pop up in another! However, nobody really believes this could actually happen.

Are UFOs, therefore, imaginary? Most scientists and many psychologists believe they are. But to people who have encountered them, UFOs are real. Many adult Americans claim to have seen a UFO. A surprising number of people think they exist.

Glossary

amateur A person who devotes time and energy to something without payment.

archaeology The scientific study of the remains, the art and dwellings, of past human life.

civilian Any person who is not a member of the armed forces or the police department.

comet A frozen ball of ice, dust, and chunks of rock with a trailing "tail" that orbits the Sun.

conclude To come to a decision after looking at the facts, or to bring something to an end.

cooperation Working with other people on a specific task.

destruction The act or the result of blowing something up, or causing terrible damage.

discernible Something that can be seen or understood, but only with some difficulty.

galaxy A group of stars and planets that are held together by gravity. There are billions of galaxies in the universe.

historian A person who studies or writes about history.

hoax Something that turns out to have been a trick. Usually a hoax is used to make people believe something that is not true.

illuminate To light up, or to make something clear.

missionary A religious person who goes to teach a particular faith to people in other countries.

personnel People who are employed by a business or other type of organization such as the military services.

primitive The earliest stages of human history, or something that is simple or basic.

psychologist A person who scientifically studies the human mind and human behavior.

radar A device that locates an object, such as an airplane, using radio waves.

radiation The sending out of a flow of particles or waves, such as X rays. Also the escape of harmful levels of energy from a nuclear power plant.

radioactive Something that is giving off harmful energy, such as fallout from a nuclear bomb.

ravine A deep, narrow valley with steep sides. Ravines are usually created by streams or rivers.

technology The study of science that has a practical use in industry.

trance A sleeplike condition of the mind while a person is awake.

Index

Further Reading

Asimov, Isaac, et al. *UFOs: True Mysteries or Hoaxes,* "Library of the Universe" series. Gareth Stevens, 1995

Emert, Phyllis R. *Monsters, Strange Dreams, and UFOs,* "Strange Unsolved Mysteries" series. Tor Books, 1990

Landau, Elaine. *UFOs,* "Mysteries of Science" series. Millbrook Press, 1995

McMurtry, Keno. *A History of Mystery: The Mystery of the Roswell UFO.* Avon, 1992

Zullo, Allan. *UFO Kids.* Troll, 1994